Tonney Ibe

Bizarre Cantillations
Seeking Redemption

Tonney Ibe

ISBN: 978-1720903291

ISBN: 1720903298

DEDICATION

To they who acknowledge the road to awareness, and those who spruce it
with earth, gravel, and tar.

Acknowledgements

I wish to thank all who have intermittently, yet constantly, prodded me all through the years to dare to make so conscious a commitment to art as to publish a collection of poems. I cannot thank you enough! The inner circle, loved ones, especially, who per the demands of the muse suffer such unintentional deprivations as are legion to highlight, thank you for understanding however grudgingly yet so encouragingly - I appreciate you, sincerely.

Through the twists and turns of a life which could only appropriately be described as normal, there have been moments of high and low. However in the course of these unassuming undulations, there is a trooping-in-and-out of passengers, who collectively move to define half a meaning to the whole insipid drudge called life. In my story, the actors are too numerous to name, except to highlight a representative few for the lot. Murni Hamzah, you are a true friend, God bless you; Aj Dagga Tolar, you are a contributor to this dull script of a poet; Omiaghocho Adechabo, an elephant of a pillar; Ricardo Antonio Garcia, of blessed memory for the double exposure in his anthologies; Solomon Okpa, for the infinite prodding year after year (laughs), thank you, sir; Jide Badmus, you are blessed! I hasten to apologise, for truncating what would surely result in an epistle in a bid to keep it simple: the memory does not fail; I thank you so much from the deepest recesses of my heart. Last but not least, I appreciate the wielders of spears, swords and what have you, who are quick to put to practice the role of villain, thank you for spurring me on the path.

CONTENTS

PREFACE

In a deeply and truly chaotic world, the very few choices for a soul in search of clarity are all enshrined in the Self. But where is the self and what is it? Too often it suffers corruption at the mercy of such esteemed definers as the earth avails, who hasten to expend the fullest weight of an all-too-limited human grasp of boundless phenomena. Perhaps in being so boundless, if a concession might be so afforded, it dares to bear a spiritual, even metaphysical, mark. Either way, what is clear enough is a somewhat sub-super element which it engenders. A little shy of sheer presumption, to conclude in the first place that the choices are few for a soul (a being really) in search of clarity, is one for history to throw around in the ring. However, still, beyond this, to declare it is found in the Self: needless to say, a-once-and-for-all phantom, dead or nonexistent entity - according to popular wisdom; brims with the benign onset of intellectual hubris, and all its attendant failures. It is acknowledged!

In any case, the self exists in the immediate space, within and without the intangible, immaterial, immeasurable psyche of mankind in a mostly unbalanced, dysfunctional relationship with the more immediate outer prism of the conceivable world. If knowledge must endure unblemished by mortal limitations, humanity - often steered by some kind of elite establishment - must learn to traverse the shallow smacks of presumptuousness.

This work does not attempt to define the Self, or to sublimate it. It merely attempts to take the kindred reader back to the inmost reaches of themselves; to shut the eyes, and in so doing open them as gateways to the truth of the being as a divine factotum for the immediate, and therefore the farther, world to thrive on a better hue of an infinite rainbow.

Bizarre Cantillations is a bipartite collection of verses comprising protests to the pseudo-natural misnomers in the human condition, and romantic confessions of love. The first part, Awareness, tackles the tragedies of the individual being upon the realisation of a bond, an unseemly bondage, with the social polity in which they exist. Perhaps the answer to real freedom is lost. However as the second part, Confessions, unfurls, it becomes clear that love is all-encompassing an ingredient for the being-self, and the world-self to flourish. It lends credence to the idea that human literature (and indeed all talent) is political in nature.

Tonney Ibe

Lagos, Nigeria

2018

I

AWARENESS

PROLOGUE

Tonney is a bird

Floating on peace neon.

Ibe was the cage!

Now I Be

A sky-bound skedaddle,

Rolling on a tumble,

Into clouds

White over blue,

Clarity -ascension into

Peace; limitation;

The mystery unseen:

Man is a bird!

My message is simple,

The a-b-c of becoming.

Your star is the sail,

It may be at half-mast

Or a botched ship

In life's vast, vast yard.

What do you do to time;

Your friend of the infinite,

When he smiles at your flaws

Yet stabs, starves and stalls

Joy in the middle of the morrow?

Twenty-four hours is insufficient!

Stop and stare, smell the roses,

Your life is all the life there is,

Alone and not alone,

In the final moment of silence,

What will be the retrospect?

From tobacco to dreams of Tobago,

The Magi of new might

 Hazard the pleasures of leaves.

No gold, frankincense nor myrrh;

But for a lone star,

Eastward and within.

A babe is born,

A prophecy long a-coming!

In the strictest of dirt;

In darkness of blood and sweat,

Upon punched keys and ink:

The impartial quill on parchment!

The Magi of new

Is a fool seeking awareness:

A loather of redemption.

Armed with wine, pipe,

And text, a desert-worthy

Camel docks on a quay

Of fresher, refreshing insight.

The babe is creation,

A weeping of font,

An affront of words.

The Magi of new is cursed!

BATTERED CAVE

In those days

My soul was Lagos,

Rugged, and funked

With the thickest and blackest

Of smog following about.

Hungry, I yawned and yawned;

Broke, I groped, hit a fine stroke,

And prayed to my last One kobo.

A European heart unsteady,

I could swim the Mediterranean,

The safest baptism to freedom.

Born into a black history;

Into the blacker annals of

Black consciousness: white

Pages stained with stigma:

Three centuries of Atlantic crossings

Shackled below decks of sty;

History could be a witch,

Tripoli a coven for the conclave.

5

Home is the Iroko's birthplace,

In hunger or insolvency,

In the most squalid of disrepair.

To survive is to die everyday

- To live and relive the chains,

The whips from the trip to hope,

Lashes lashing gashes gushing

Stale blood as I walked

The runway to Kidnap Central.

I recoil within the battered cave,

An assaulted black fool.

To hell with the greener grass,

On this rock I shall fast

Till death, my friend,

Pours me the tallest glass.

THE LOST ONES

Seven billion souls

Walk this earth

Of snakes and snails.

A soul must walk,

Limp-legged, proudly;

Wistfully, disinterestedly;

It must travel

- No birth a berth!

From gravitation

To levitation,

The epic image of God

Attains to relevance.

Every spirit on the greens,

Is a billion beautiful

Possibilities: Laughter

Like lilies leaving love

Laced on paths yet not

Encountered to flower

Fated coincidences,

Hate to devour

In the hour.

But life's not all veggies!

There are seasons:

A bleeding, a healing;

A leaking, a sealing;

A bursting, containing;

A shedding and growing;

An Ebbing and flowing:

An infinite seeking

-The unconscious yearning,

From tailspin to spin

A bluesy ball in covert orbit.

The last of the lost is unseen;

The loss of the last is unseen,

Of the seven billion souls

Who walk the Earth?

The lost ones are blessed!

HOME

Just like that,

A submarine in open water,

I dive: I dive!

Under attack,

Crashing on the Canyon walls.

It's not the ocean blue,

It's me in me finding me.

Away, down and aft,

I bow to bind my bruises,

Salt and pepper,

Lime on the baggy grime

Of a floundered soul.

I shriek, Sméagol, dark eagle

Pitted against contradictions

In my drooped and dying Janus.

I'm lost at sea,

I'm lost at sea,

I'm lost at sea;

Counting on monsters

To navigate a way home.

Down below,

Thirty thousand feet

In the deep of my soul,

I cower, fret and fritter,

To the images of doom

Flashing between dimensions.

Halfway there, here,

I must shut my ears,

Shaking feet and phalanges,

Fish-man, fish-bait,

And picture home.

I picture home!

RELEASE

Maybe our scars are different,

But we have both bled:

The inmost dwelling,

A haunted house.

Scraped on the keel,

This body hikes on its heel

In search of the infamous hill,

Where peace burns eternally:

It is El Dorado!

My wounds are vales oozing

Steam, hot lava, and mild tremors;

My life, a festival for flies

To feed as I bleed

And brood, and break.

I have contemplated in the dark,

The devil's deed

One time too many.

I saw heaven flaked in rum

Running from a crystal decanter,

A solemn wish to die drunk,

And stay dead until a waking.

So why cloak the gash

Dealt by life's lash

Under checkered smiles?

Cry, Scream,

Burst at the seams!

Maybe our scars are different,

But pain is a universal brunt.

Yours I've carried before,

Mine you might feel sometime.

If only sleep slaked worries,

The monotonous honking of Lorries

Might scurry into the distance.

If only the roadmap to clarity,

Was more than a dream in death?

It would all be for naught.

Mining the black dot

That is a lifelong commitment,

I am crying, screaming,

And bursting at the seams!

A new scar is underway.

A POET'S PRAYER

Accept me,

An angel with broken wings,

A villain of my own soul,

A mad essence in a cool suit...

I am...,

A stargazer from a sad view,

A lord of the house of pain.

Muse and muses!

I pray thee,

Avail me the bosom of truth

-A gladiatorial quill!

Let my art drink

Of the fountain of youth,

And shout upon the mountains:

"Ponce de Leon! Ponce de Leon!"

Rest me with trees,

A passenger seeking solace

-A pitcher of tents!

Here I am- a fool, your fool,

With herb, pen, and fire;

13

To burn my rubble of ignorance.

On some days

I doubt the higher purpose!

But fuel these doubts,

I pray thee,

To a glorious combustion,

Muse and muses!

Take me into your grace,

A teller of truths;

Oh Onyia! Private goddess!

Make love to my mind,

-Again, again, and again-

Until I'm grey and feeble;

Sowing the seeds of awareness

Of neither clairvoyance;

Neither reason nor rhymes,

But a mission to change lives:

To make earth a better home!

I pray thee,

Trust me with the sword of truth

- A knight of humanism.

Amen.

MINE

I am standing on a minefield,

I am a mine,

I am mine,

Death in a sleeper.

Silence!

And kaboom!

History hugs prophecy,

Fate is a tease.

TO LEAVE, A LEAF OR A DREAM

It is a long night, featuring several dream sessions, long enough for an assault of the colourless leaf, something like a soul, radiating with the spark of the spirit.

In one such dream, the statue of Buddha could unwrap its legs from the ascetic grip of the guru, and tie faith with the Coat of Arms in Unity, Peace, and Progress. It could kiss the eagle and the kiss shall set it free, free from the might of her hubris and the cast image of her lifeless station. It smiled towering high above ground, a plush shadow of grace printed on the twin tame horses as they scamper into reality. Once and forever, stagnation does not become a country living a lie of plenty, the sacred truth bound and sealed, proscribed, in the belly of the Caucus.

Some dream and dreams do not ask permission! Not even daydreams and their comic relief which litter banana peels on the runway of social consciousness in time for the human motorcade, a sheep-like citizenry treading like zombies the slippery soapbox of effects: It is either a rise or a fall, but whether either the destiny of the stem is fulfilled.

To be stuck with a dream, an undying Goliath is the choice to live, in dreams or the great sleepwalk which every leaf is doomed to suffer.

I shall walk away from it all, riding slowly on the bark of a dream, the dream, a leaf, one way or another, the exit is ineluctable.

THE POEM

The poem's an old tree,

An Oak of sorts!;

Leaves on its branches.

In the passage of time,

There's a dropping:

The voyage to dust;

A trip to earth of roots

To the chronicles

-The corpus of souls

On the road to awareness;

Into helpless immortality.

The poem is whole,

A collection of poems

Moving in simulation,

Up and down spaces

Within its thick trunk.

Every leaf is a poet!

Dull goblets of sap;

Saplings of the sacral,

Springing on the clock.

A poet is home within,

A leaf of consciousness,

Humility into the night!

If humanity is the sea,

The poet is a promontory

For the splashing;

For the clinging;

For the resting of

Waters of the human spirit.

But there are creepers!

A creeper is a charlatan,

A wily weaver of words,

A thudding heart of mind

Shorn of new nuance.

It is the snake snaking

To the very top of leaves:

A conceited ambition!

The poem's a gift at war,

An aviary; a poultry.

It sings the many tales

Of eagles and peacocks:

Tales of flight; flight of tales,

In the falling to dust,

In wilting to oblivion.

There's hope in the tree:

The poem, an unlikely pair.

LOST

Lost

In the noble pursuit,

The drudge of being human,

In suspended animation.

The reality seems

Far and nigh,

Like death echoes.

It is vanity!

The drudge seeking meaning.

A spouse, a child, a life!

Strange is the cycle,

Tired of being human.

The drudge yet again

Makes madness desirable.

A stretcher in bedlam,

In contrast, appealing;

A countdown to the weeping

- the return to dust

Hanging like hellish haloes.

Lost in the art

Of being human;

Lost to the meaning of life,

Loss at a loss!

It is vanity...

It is vanity!

She wields the pen,

The drudge,

The drudge yet again:

To have life and be alive

- A lofty antithesis -

Being human at the gallows!

BABALAWO

In the clear-blue born

Of day, before the selfish

Squealing of the roosters;

On the sapless hours of

Deities, where oil lamps

Once the dark deprived;

Tapped from super-conscious

Traps of the half death,

Wakened to offer libation

Upon ghastly images of

Divine figurines who

In solitude, sing songs

In ancient, nonexistent

Tongues of Truth.

Draped in black

- A chameleon of doom -

He strums the fluffy feathers

Of the mischievous Eshu,

Baying echoed praises

Into vaticinal palms, which

Defy heavy wily winds,

To reassert his fealty

- Then softly to sleep!

He well knows that

To doubt, is to believe

At a slower firmer pace;

And to believe all too

Readily might be doubt

in a yielding shroud

- He is a believer! A

Potent vessel of hope;

A cultural curator,

Healing, cursing, coursing!

Appeasing the witch herd

- Sacrifices for the snare

Of supernatural stench,

Of Sicknesses and false health -

Pouring from the cauldron,

In his miraculous mouth,

The heat of vengeance

Into envious offenders,

23

Who seek the unjust

Slaughter of happy victims.

Shoved by the times,

Behind the mainstream of

Events, he remains a

Light in strange shadows.

TO FEAR

Fear no one,

But fear all the same.

Step out of yourself

And see the foundation:

You have you to fear!

The fear of yourself

Is the first book of wisdom.

THE CITY

A twist in the fog

Might hope to usher

In a bright new day:

The city needs light!

She's a big black bum

Posing as a Swiftian giant.

How the mighty have fallen!

A harem of royals,

Drunk on privilege,

Her body politic is

A bazaar of lesions.

But she must do make-up,

Clad in starched Agbada,

Palm-on-cheek snoring

In the comity of cities.

Within her bosom,

Two great rivers fork

Into a brilliant yawn.

Her tail is a trigger,

The hub of many a wick,

A conurbation of creeks

Begging that the ceilings fall.

It was half a century

Of rape by the definers,

A splash of incest,

Now she jerks off to

An elegant world viewing,

Shamelessly and proudly!

A poster child of the pseudo,

The sun might dare

To risk a western rising,

But to hear her sing again

The songs of reverse.

And so the flame unbridled,

Upon her gentle Zuma,

Long left to the elements,

Has begun to root.

Every hour is for destiny,

She must nature become.

History is a man inspired,

And he a god possessed.

The city is a summary blurb,

The blurb a bubble;

Her abhorrence for dialogue

Is a dearth of wisdom,

For might is right, or slight!

She's a corpse amnesiac,

Infernal carrion:

Two hundred million strong.

BEHIND AND BEYOND

He locks himself in,

Cut off from the world,

A contemporary Crusoe;

A subject of his own psychosis.

His madness is rich!

From a thin crack on the white wall,

All the noises from without

Seep in like a Sinatra record,

A soft, feeling, sensible tune.

The dream is dreamed,

On the same bed in the same room,

A livid, eerie dream of grandeur;

From his pregnant head

Upon that same passionate pillow.

The dream is real enough,

But reality is beyond those walls.

Yet the madness of the multitude,

The fumes, and the delinquency...,

They keep him locked in,

Cut off from the world-

A mental case of greatness!

Sooner than later,

He must realise

That half of being alive,

Is to die someday.

He must soon leave the room,

That same Eden,

Where the plan was conceived!

Before the final Eden,

A Paradise beyond,

Beyond the narrow box;

Freedom like ashes upon wind,

Ricocheting to the same multitude,

Behind and beyond.

KPOMO BIRD

She flies about the Hindu Kush

In her malevolent mind,

A computer bird steeped in

Numbers, calculating projections

Of a few worthwhile morsels in

The nest. From the milk-teeth

Age, life forced her feet to

Strive, and tread upon mountains.

The taller she grew,

The higher the climb, but then

Came Kpomo: wings at suckle time,

A protruding chest - fated gifts -

To ease with breezes the

Listless drifts of her destiny.

It is a true story: the

Sales pitch of a beautiful bird,

With wily wings of kpomo -

Round and robust - a fitting fact

For freaky men of means.

For in her gait, all passions

Bear testament to lecherousness:

Kpomo on her head tray,

Kpomo in her poultices,

Kpomo in her soiled soul,

And everywhere in between:

Kpomo is a kind of food!

She has many a prisoner,

But is a prisoner herself

Stuck beyond wing-flapping

In massive kpomo walls.

She is a kind of food!

A SIGN

If hope is real,

Gift me a slim slice

Polished with fresh jam.

Let the spirits sing a

Jackson cover as I sip

Some spirit connecting to

The higher purpose spontaneously.

At least give me a sign!

Take these red eyes of mine,

Which have seen suffering

Like a Lagos evening traffic; But give

Not them to the man born blind.

Avail me Whitman and Okigbo,

Father, son, and grandson seated

By the sea bank petting the

Pipe pregnant with ideas.

A pinch of Pound's lucky dementia,

To the sour soup that is my life,

33

Perhaps it might make a difference!

Show me love through God's sight,

And this earth from man's mind.

Give me a heated soul,

For harmattan is mighty nigh.

If hope were real, these suicidal

Streams would cease to flow,

And the debris with them.

LELEWEYN

All so true,

Soft, she flows from the depths,

Every drop is a chapter

On the somber pages.

She's a dear friend,

Sweet company in misery.

Never missing her,

An entrance after,

I do, I say I do.

As fire to my bones,

And power to my being,

I feel Leleweyn, yet

I do not call for her.

LAST WARNING

Oga, take your rifle out of my face,

Pause a moment,

Do you realise that you are the hell

Which awaits us all?

Fear cannot be better than love!

I'm neither bloody nor a bloody civilian;

I am the payer and you the payee;

I am your procurer!

But what gracious irony

That you clock the wooden threat

Baying the scream-a-scream infinitely.

Turn off the damn siren,

My brother is in gaol

But no Madiba, how does he emerge

From the shackles of your walls,

And re-assimilate into the outer prison?!

We see the truth in your lies,

We realise,

We sympathize

With the doom in your pride:

Your pride is our cries?

It comes swiftly before the fall

From glory, Everest to the vale

Where wailings are flowers stale

Fertile graves, fertile graves

Bones of the oppressor,

Engraved by the commons.

Where's justice when you shoot

Like practice the souls of innocents!;

Nailing innocence at the stake,

The stakes dragged up a notch:

This guillotine sharpened for reckoning

- Naija remembers!

Bleeding ceaselessly thro' the ruptured

Arteries of national consciousness,

The army of vengeance files,

Fusing on common ground,

Silently gearing for revolution

As violence of the alecs

Taketh by force the harvest,

The plunder, pillage and conquest.

We shall smell a fresh paradigm,

When the will emboldens, cutting

Short this hiatus of commonsense,

To pick up your toys of death

And deal to you joys in your coin,

You who are hard of heart,

Who lay to charge suffering

Upon suffering upon suffering,

Twisting heaven into Hades

These twin horses that is hungry

On a green patch of plenty,

The coat of arms armed to the hilt;

Of mass murders, unarmed robberies,

And extrajudicial killings.

Who kills, steals, and destroys,

But 'Lux Ferre' and their underlings?!

The wage shall be a page

Hoisted in unmitigated rage,

You, you, and you

Cast in red,

The graven image of dread

Messed up for history

That no more shall it endure,

The dealing of fear and death

Dealt by the Horsemen.

Your word is trash!

Your metals of black

We shall cease.

Sad and confident,

One with the majority,

This manifesto is a warning,

Oga, take your rifle out of my face.

HALF A SOUL

What do I know,

I am half a boy,

Half a soul, half a puppet,

About whose neck's noosed

By all the intercontinental cords.

The inner man is a cockroach

Cursed, unaware of its ilk.

Dimmed by the old chains,

History forges novel ones:

Invisible, firmer, tighter shackles.

Half a fiction, I abjure the earth,

I denounce the continents,

I deny the many-coloured flags.

The journey to fullness;

The grave or shadow of the casket,

Is the breaking of the fetters

And prisons of emigration.

But what do I know,

I am only half a toy!

BABYLON FLIGHT

I'm a bird at heart,

A legend lost in translation,

Soaring around - no borders in sight.

I'm a radiant Bird of Paradise,

Taken to a rat race in a tough world,

So far off from Eden's watersides.

Above and beyond the lofty clouds,

I revel in my reverie revelation(s)

Of emptiness below, and loud.

"Holy Mount Zion!" A sinner chants,

"When shall my eagle be unleashed,

The prophecy made flesh and fat?"

I'm some bird - or so it seems,

But I forget sometimes I could fly,

Little wonder I cross my deserts on foot.

From this horizon to the next,

From our Africa to the captors' coven,

Faith has put my wings to the test!

BECOMING

The man becomes a boy,

And longs to escape no further.

REALITY CHECK

Today, the flag is at a standstill,

The wind is hot, cold, and strange.

It's a dawn, old and dreary!

Anger was a fad before the

Cock crowed, cried, and cracked its spine;

It is swift for bird and beast, monk and

Mallam, swift! Right now a soft trigger.

Wailing voices are creaking

In the range of rage, each one a G.I.

In spirit, gearing for a revolution. But

There's no proper way to scream out loud!

Noise is music, and speakers are booming.

Today Trust has broken a neck riding

On sensibilities - quantum - in a quandary.

It is a red one, although the moon is

High at nine ante meridian.

Food is scarce, joy is dare, throats are thirsty

But eyes are rife with tears rife with truth,

A deluge of a mummy bursting at the slightest

Provocation. Today is a good day for thoughts,

Yet a dangerously bad, bad one for hope

Who has stripped to the skin, scraped to the bone,

Baking in a hell broth, chowder for strife.

Never anticipated nor dreaded enough,

Today has been long a-coming.

There are shots fired everywhere, except

From the barrel of a gun, but who can survive

Without armor? The dead are dying fresh deaths,

Destiny is presiding, and viciously adjudicating.

Today, all eyes have seen a failed state.

It is no ordinary day!

ZAINAB

She is in shrouds,

A prisoner of extremists' philosophy;

A walking, breathing tent!

She feels lesser but is more,

Genuflecting to mortal divinities

At every passing and waking.

Although her head and body bow,

Her soul remains unbowed,

Escaping unnoticed, those fatwa

And pseudo-transcendental dogmas,

Embracing the obvious truths.

She is in torment,

For her activist dreams may

Never leave the departure lounge.

Anchored in the desert sands;

Berated by bigotry of the sexes;

Perhaps flogged at the city square,

In a recapped and recurring nightmare,

She steals her dagger,

47

Ready to do herself in.

Zainab is a human being!

She's soul and bone and blood,

A victim of such timeless euphemisms,

As Nazism, fascism, communism,...

Wait! She stares at a desk,

which used to seat her holy book

Before it caught the flames:

Those flames of her reaffirmation!

And as the smoke seeped

Into the naked sun,

So did the chains and imposed guilts.

She is a wo-man,

Brilliant, enterprising, ambitious - spiritual!

Her legs are still, but full of soul.

They run from the annexation

Of her rich essence and spirit,

To life, liberty, and the pursuit of happiness.

Zainab is a human being!

An assault on her,

Is an assault on you!

Be her voice!

TRAUMA

On some days,

Perfection is I seated

Idly, donning no more than

The disaster of nakedness.

I'm yet to find God,

In between short breaks

From hunger and pain;

To smile from within

The borrowed inn

Of my lean soul,

Where I pay no bills

For light, water. or comfort.

I've paid my last Naira,

Yet here I sit

Sweating like Africa

Flooded by her seven rivers.

I know not how to cry,

For I was taught to laugh

Till my dying breath:

Laughter is a shield

From the nine plagues!

But so what?

What's so special about

Spaces stilted with straits?

I challenge Azrael with tears

From the last drying oasis

Of my sad story.

Come whisk me away,

From this social trauma,

To the Father

- Nowhere near paradise!

GRACE AND RECKONING

Life takes its toll on us yet it gives,

Year after year it brings in the sheaves,

Per our mortality we must give thanks,

Knowing that sorrow and joy have banks.

I'm a benefactor of unusual grace,

Standing as adamantium fray after furnace,

Against the paucity of tacit truth(s)

- Such introverted atrocities that I loot.

I think, therefore I could become,

However fettered my soul nor steep my sum.

My words, my thoughts, my ideation!

My pain then is not without explanation.

So in the heat of the long trials of life,

Solace shall find me always and ever rife,

A dreamer with little more than a dream,

A conscious quill scribing ream after ream.

Could the world be spirited enough for humility,

The gamble of the scramble, or its futility?

To be or not to be wealthier or cleverer,

The only wealth worth craving is life forever!

THE ESCAPE

It is easy to go the way of hate,

To water a grudge till it blossoms,

Shedding its leaves in autumn;

But it must be hard,

To be the bull's eye

Of bias, grudge or prejudice;

To be different;

To speak Latin in Swaziland,

Leaning on the edge of collapse.

So why do we not love enough?

It must be decried!

How true are the tears shed,

At the casting of the earth

When we had an age but failed

- To forgive and sap our egos-

To seek forgiveness; or say 'hello'?

When the money comes,

Will your soul be simpler or subtler?

54

The Lies of a kin here,

There, betrayal of a friend.

We canonise our moralities

In the acts of judgment,

Conveyed by sour platitudes;

Falling short of judging our own selves.

We clothe betrayal in a smile,

Smiling through life's vicissitudes,

Trumpeting little deeds at the slightest.

From a penthouse I stare down,

At myself and his excesses

- Though my pitfalls are my neighbour's,

For we are all human -

And aye! I acknowledge, that:

"I am a serf, sick of serfdom,

A helot of my own devices!

I long to escape from myself,

Much as I long to long for it;

But where do I go from here

When the safety of its sweetness endures?"

I should like to know too

What premise justifies envy.

Is it where it shelves on a heart?

Is it okay to be greedy

(To deprive another

The pleasure of gratification),

If I am not stingy?

Yet I find that I envy sometimes

- An Oliver Twist in my own right-

And detest myself for it!

So a white door stares,

From across the darkness.

Its rims shimmer

With a swagger.

All that I am,

And all that I could be,

I would renounce

To walk past that door:

To transcend myself!

For to be human alive,

Is a somewhat

Benign form of slavery.

I'm not long for the escape!

HOPE AUDACIOUS

Someday home shall be home,

Without the absence of peace;

Without the excess of peace,

Someday home shall be home!

Canaries creaking in the rear,

No more vultures in a vacuum,

No more vacuums, no more inertia;

Adults teaching children to laugh,

Once again a joyful carapace to caption.

Someday history will be made, to

Archive the truths of shameful past,

The blood of kin long desecrated

Might forgive, with luck, forget

Betrayal under big guns' civil seals.

Someday, perhaps someday, suspicion

Might receive euthanasia to sleep

Immortality, never to interfere, never

To partake of sociopolitical baths.

Someday after the Lost Generation

Has traversed its Dead Sea account,

Youths may yet hazard genuine

Smiles, when the gray and feeble

Relegate senility to geriatric homes,

Far away from policy bombs

Ticking in the public foray.

Somehow teachers would teach truly,

Posterity held captive by freedom,

And the ideals of an intent voyage.

Someday, someday in time unknown,

All hands on deck- fraud to haul overboard!

Surplus food for mind, soul and body, as

-Empty bellies banter not of greatness-

So when the harvest comes round,

Dirge or not, we welcome a new dream, and

Violence by motley armed uniforms

Could cease to assault the people,

The fascist squealing of Stentor,

Romping and rumbling never ever again-

Strand by strand, peeled off;

Strand by strand, disarmed;

Strand by strand re-armed,

With truth like fresh palm wine,

Wisdom to discern light from brightness

Then darkness, and conscience to end

Oppression of mind and consciousness.

In time, the fears of damnation,

Fanaticism, complexes, and godist obsessions,

Might hibernate on trivial spectra.

The essential seed of spiritual thought,

Resonating solely in a pure human love,

Spread not in words but constant reflex:

One love across the vast society!

If right is right, and wrong- wrong,

Someday home shall be home!

FAITH

Seated on a sofa;

Torn between faith and reality,

And the malodorous dualism;

I wiggle back and forth

Like a missionary pendulum

In search of space.

From birth to the brewery,

Memories of morality waver

- Fresher than my rebellion -

To the stick and sermon thereafter.

I pause, and prod, and pass!

Tethered to a bull's testicles,

My soul screams in muted attempts,

Splintered amongst choices:

Spiritual choices!

Shall I kneel, or, bend low,

To flesh favour from the fates?

Do I look upon the majesty,

Or shut my windows to the world?

Today, offerings of beating hearts I give,

I give..., I give, to espy the rainbow.

How far I have traveled,

From the Martian sands of dogmatism,

Yet so parallel to my vanity!

I am torn

Between Intricacy and simplicity,

A sacrificial soul at its spoliation.

In quietude I seek shelter,

From the war within,

Fleeing from the war without,

And the cosmopolitan blitzkrieg of belief.

Tanks are advancing,

To a bombastic holocaust.

Bible across the Qur'an;

Torah across the Gita;

Belief across unbelief;

Sacredness across unorthodoxy,

Gearing for the crash finale.

In sapped smiles,

At the grotesque scenery,

I'm resolved to fortification

- African and proud -

As razors thrust into action,

Blazing along Ifa lines,

From head to toe:

The black ash to the rescue!

Seated here on a sofa,

Having voyaged between worlds,

Within this wanton world;

I hew to a saddening script.

The pretentious ball of wax,

Is melting by the heat

Of its denizens.

The flames of faith are burning!

A KISS

There's nothing so simple as a kiss.

I wouldn't trade it for honey;

For a pillow of dove feathers;

Nor a life of goat meat pepper soup

And foamy ice cold beer.

I love to kiss, to live the

Imagined movement of lips,

Pure and natural -promising

Like pen to paper,

The smell of ink;

Birth of the unknown

From a known, planned

Intentional kiss. It is the

Complex session of simplicity,

That an idea might labour

Into a vision, a mission, and

History becomes flesh

- A nation for instance,

Without senseless fractures,

Nor rifts, and ancestral gashes:

That a diverse specimen of

Souls might learn to kiss,

And learn from its twists and

Turns a second coming of

Seasons, equinoxes, solstices,

And no little lengths of laughter.

From there to learn, and teach

Posterity and beyond,

That nothing's so simple as a kiss.

PAIN

How real is pain?

Is he whole or halved?

Does he hurt or is he hurt?

Do you see him in a mirror of grief?

Does he rain in a single teardrop?

They say fire hurts? Nonsense!

And so a foot bleeds indigo streams,

Flesh dancing the rumba in iridescence

At the dawn of imminent effects;

It hurts, yes! But is it painful?

Is he in the feel or in the deal?

No legion of affectations

Could ever alter the wealth within!

Drenched in amber,

A soul at war with itself

- Partaker of the games -

Might reap a plenteous harvest,

As the darkness smears the cross;

Resolving alas that pain and hurt,

Are twain siblings at odds.

Only Saturday I was badly hurt,

In the pangs of some emotion,

My fidgety fingers flowing,

On a streak of beige rhythms,

The feeling so unsure....

Such is the pain,

To know what pain is!

Tonney Ibe

THE FIRST DAY

From infancy, life availed

A gift, the gift, a path to the sun.

It was well and good,

The second day.

On the flipping of a page,

The mind drew upon the

Symbiosis of sun and moon,

That in darkness there's light;

The third day.

Rain could drop,

A sky of heavy clouds

Tightened to trick thirsty throats,

Wet the arid fields of fleas,

Hello to livestock,

But not the alfresco trader

Whose shade is the promise of

A better day in elusive tomorrows.

The fourth day.

Both heart and lips sing,

Between them a few light years.

Their song is different.

This the soul has known.

The last day

.

The funeral is a feast,

Do not wake me up,

I have had my fill of feasts.

The first day.

PARCHMENTS

Lift me up with spikes of hyssop,

Hurl me with a forklift of chalice,

Let me rain upon the red fields,

Sprouts of grape uncelebrated.

Let me flow as fiction on parchment,

Lift me up, tear me down,

Paint me, a chirping Picasso

Unflinching as the canary blues.

Let me emerge a vineyard connoisseur

- A savant of the solvent arts -

An army of letters in internship.

Take me as I am, a fiction;

Free me, put me to the prints,

Throw in the towel, polish the flint.

Swallow me, a pill of consciousness,

And forget the drudgery of ignorance.

Oh drag me into Valhalla,

Where Odin presides upon vintage.

You are there now,

In the fifth circle of truth,

Bend the ciboria lopsidedly,

Stain these parchments of iridescence.

From your mind to the next,

Cantillations sung at your bar mitzvah;

Immortality is only the beginning!

ODE OF ODES

What is the motherland,

But a tunnel vision of (home)

Home seen through a clean shot

At the heart of a fallen comrade?

Where's the motherland?

In an elusive Oasis?

Beside the abounding groves

Of palm and jacaranda,

Against the defiant cries

Of scared monkeys;

Surely the desert is far off!

So where is it?

It must not be in this portrait

Which conceals hunger and hate

With resplendent colours,

Where Babelian monuments

Overlook sour thatched roofing.

The waters are bleak

- Black as Kaku -

And as they body forth

Into the reality of the motherland,

She lets go of all resistance,

Persistent for instance,

Like the sheer will of violence

Unleashed by the greens and blacks,

Plundering all sanity and history;

She spreads her mutilated behind

- Mottled by the motley madness -

For the umpteenth assault.

There goes the motherland!

Far yet nigh; dead yet alive;

Gang-raped in drunken turns,

There, beyond reclamation;

There, away from the kingdom,

In the kingdom come:

An endangered utopia in the sun!

Loyal is the lion to the pride,

But a groom to his bride?

The tribe, kindred, and clan,

Pull rank against the motherland.

Who is deserving of fealty?

Her udders solemnly sag,

Torpid with the milk of progress:

Who suckles of the froth?

Through the cracks of a carrion,

The scarlet image of hope

Stinks, sticking to the script,

But even hope becomes weary.

Doubt is looming on the plains!

The essence of brotherhood,

A fact of life in peril,

It is doubly doubted!

So Cain and Abel,

With the force of an alien tongue;

And a hammer of resentment,

Clash in the sun where

Utopias rise for the setting-

The Animus shines brightly,

Across the Savannah straights:

Let no man put asunder!

What mama and papa

Bled incessantly for,

In the heat of ruthless resolve;

In the fury of determination,

Under hellish hailstorms

Of machine fire;

Under the ingenious contrivance

Of Ogbunigwe in her frightful majesty

- Let no man put asunder!

In the tunnel vision of freedom,

Even the bravado to exist;

In plenty or squalor,

Joy comes at sundown,

Over footnotes of mutual animosity;

She comes jamming

Onyeka's 'One love' on repeat:

Joy comes at the green flash!

So that brush and ink,

Might fly slowly but surely

Upon canvass;

75

Stroke after splash,

Converting the artistic mess

Of the messianic masters,

Into a painting of home.

Though blood and bigotry,

Have scaled east through west,

The sun still shines!

Amidst friendly fires;

And the booties of public service,

Green complements white!

A generation is born,

To fill the charred arms

Of a great and undying mother:

Lions and lioness

In the black shrubbery-

She beckons ever forgivingly.

The gods gather at noon,

Sounding the unctuous horn,

To the dolphin and the shark

In all men:

Let no man put asunder!

The waters are flowing,

They flow to the cleansing;

To the quenching of thirst;

To the drying of tears,

Tears shed for crying sake.

Oh mother!

Fathers weep as mothers peep,

Children are tired of yawning

-Better a belch than a yawn.

The means matter no more;

The end becomes an end in itself,

But the kingdom is come;

The motherland is come,

Let no man put asunder!

SUNSET AT DAWN (FOR DR MIKE, ON HIS PASSING)

Life is a splash of ink

Upon parched earth,

The rough begrudged sink

Into sure frowns and laughter.

Not every morrow is certain,

Though the sun shines

It is setting,

Each second a mime

Of the alarm

Without occasion.

Death is a new beginning,

Marked by tears and retreat,

The end of the sweet

And pleasurable moments

Amongst loved ones soon to be hurt.

Although tears tarry,

A star has gone home,

To seek the face of God,

This home has passed into

Memory

Shattered below the earth-shed

Within a few feet of clay and root,

The awful truth

At dawn.

A rock is off to blossom

A smiling constellation

Looking down, counting down the

Time

To burst into a flame

Speeding across our sky

A shooting star

For us to make a wish,

Any wish but to have you back,

A gallant soldier, physician, Father, human being,

In our heavy hearts

Like you never left.

It is

Like you never left, papa.

METAMORPHOSIS

Before now, she was a fresh fruit,

Fine, ripe, and clearly forbidden.

She was in the eyes of men,

A treasure trough pregnant with

Prospects ready for a contravention.

Contravened, she flew of her own

Volition, as high as butterflies go,

A wisher with one wish, and one alone:

To re-emerge a caterpillar protected

By a legion of legs moving in faith

That Fate brings herself to the sun.

She is an old passenger pigeon now,

A graying lock of tresses to attest

To her proud collection of insight,

And a life lived on the left lanes.

She sings the caveat symphony,

To fresh fruits, emphasizing to butterflies,

Seated on the front porch painting

Blurry portraits of old passenger pigeons.

She well knows that time is of the essence.

Tonney Ibe

MOMENT OF TRUTH

In this moment [of silence],

Silence is speaking in tongues.

No longer at ease,

She registers her discontent

In the offing of truths

- Visceral truths!

This moment necessitates meditation,

Tricky tick after tock,

Mind is overtaken (overtaxed)

By trance and recollections,

As a deluge in a cup.

This nebulous moment is eclipsed

By itself.

The moment of the moment,

Like a shadow behind light,

Is exacted in a black blur.

In this moment,

The future is losing hope,

And humour; and future.

It is one for the chroniclers,

Long snoring in starvation.

While hands shiver

From psychal schizophrenia,

The only record worth saving,

Becomes lost and found

In the feckless moment:

The same moment, when

Today retires wearily

- A veteran of involuntary wailing.

Silence is singing a song!

Mouths are yawning concurrently,

As teeth gnash and grit,

Drooling to a disgusting apogee.

"What's the essence of a life

Bereft of moments of spirit?"

Even dogs dare to chant in falsetto!

It's a moment of absurdity;

And stupidity swimming counter-clockwise.

In this moment of bleakness,

Silence is speaking in tongues!

WITHIN

I'm in deep, an infested corn stalk,

A repented cannibal...,

I am...in...deep!;

An abandoned worker bee, patching

Up thee, a deserted shot-up beehive.

I'm in deep in the rump of my soul,

Licking like a Siamese cat, the greenish

Dirt off, the shabby shirt off, my naked

Self; abused, assailed, maimed, and

Marginalized - fair assaults they would

Be, if the essence wasn't thought less.

I'm deep, under a snail-stone,

In the crevice where earthworms bleed,

Reciting Old Catholic hymns of parochial

Tender, wary of kisses upon my cautious

Earlobes. Shall I emerge from within the

Palm trunk in my palm wine stupor of

Reflections? It is safer for now in the deep

Of formatted memories starting anew, the

Scepter and wand, poised to take on Earth

In her ceremonious imperfections....

Everything is an irony, everything is

Contrapuntal! From behind the castle

Fort, emotional offensives are launched

By friendly faces, familial, familiar with

The nooks and corners.

Enough is well enough!

ELUSION OF THE SELF

The aftermath of religious enterprise:

The masting and merchandising of man;

Is the slippery spreading of ideas

From East through West,

The thrust of the trusts of thought

In tangible or intangible ideation,

To cast bright light they say

On the twilight of dim civilizations:

Oblivious of the knowledge of caveats,

The price of encroachments

Is not without silence of the self.

At Runnymede, the hallmark of liberty

Was marked thus for the ages

- Freedom of a common people,

From centuries of generational serfdom.

Under the star of Elohim,

The death of all the old gods

From Saxony to Scandinavia,

In the annals of European cosmologies,

To christen each day of the week;

Each day an evergreen triumph,

For the birth at Bethlehem

To gain traction without gainsay.

In the wake of Auschwitz, the

Concentration of Concentration Camps,

And historic gulags of death

Caged to capture a futuristic caption:

A museum, but only forgotten memories

Riding on the premise of Babylonia

- Babylon of The Book -

Fractured along the colour bar.

For the waging and justifying of wars;

The gutting and gassing of denizens:

The genocidal leanings of pogroms.

For if the face of Truth is bashed in

With pelts painted with blood

And sweat, and crowned with thorns;

Posterity must do makeovers

-In the spirit of Fulani memoration -

By reparations in decapitation;

And so all of the Orisha

Should by default melt away,

From Ife to Sambisa,

Into six feet of the ignored Chi,

Or sixty-six feet of native land

To be drilled and pumped for oil

- All for national self-glorification.

On the crest of civilization:

The felling and clearing of flora;

The animal world retracts further inwards,

So that in the fated indoctrinations

- By whim and whip -

Which makes of men proud proselytes,

Hawking imperialism and perfection

On public buses in the haze

And daze of metropolitan madness:

The benign braggadocio of evangelism,

Sailing on threats of imminent perdition;

God reclines within inner man!

The Self is not dead,

It could never pass away,

Like Earth the walking ball:

The indissoluble factor of time.

OGUN

From beyond the bounds of flesh,

Your might is notorious;

Your voice clinks as battle ready

Swords against the gift of brotherhood.

A mighty palm with myriad heads,

You command mortal libation

In the supremacy of silence.

An incontestable deity,

Your peace flies across the hills.

At your divine bosom

Schnapps and Palm oil are snoozing,

Hanging like a forgotten beauty

- like nature in its element!

You are Ogun!:

Lord of dagger and dove

- A kaleidoscope of morality -

Weaver of carrot and stick.

The offerings of blood and bone,

Are as balm upon your bark

Black as you are, with fronds

Braided and braiding astride

Your magnificence and mystique;

Your fatalism and benediction!

You undo the locks,

Appease paths unseen,

Bulldozing a star into greatness;

But your vengeance is atomic,

Silently inflicted to the sum

Of an angelic pogrom.

When broken kolas dance

To your telekinetic Metallica,

The message is resounded

From immeasurable depths,

Into a tasking task or lesson.

Yoruba lord of the Iron,

Lord of the sundown,

Take salt, kola, and snail;

Take Palm oil

- And the sacrificial breath -

Bathe in the reddish lather.

The libation is yours!

DAUNTLESS

When death comes let it be swift,

When life comes, sword out of sheath,

When darkness brings friendship,

Be not afraid, be not afraid.

Death comes,

Then life comes;

Darkness comes,

Then light comes;

Man comes along

A mangled pole of wax

Marshaled on this here alley

-Feet on thin ice,

The slippery slope upon the exit.

Fear is a factor,

Courage the tractor.

Doubt is a bow,

Belief the arrow;

The spirit an origami

From divine palms folded

To earth the green parched porch,

A soul in chains the slow slosh,

Tongue for profession:

Red carpet of mind

Harnessed to spiritual ideologies

Doctrines of whip

- The soured swollen parentage.

Come forth into mainstream,

Aware that silk meets draft,

And wax the eternal fire.

The soul must breathe at last,

Be not afraid;

The soul must breathe at last.

Come what may,

Infirmities from the night,

The curse of Job,

The blessings of Tafari;

The soul must breathe at last:

Be not afraid!

ODACHI

Odachi - her name - a nation

Prone to fail; she's a strenuous

Exercise in incorrigible excesses.

What's beauty without brains,

But snow in the Kenyan safari?

A WMD in sleep mode

Crafted by a shrewish mother,

A soviet man of Idoma land,

A lifetime of hearing yet crying,

And too little butter for fries.

There was Delilah in the play

Which may never hazard

A dénouement; she's a rapper,

With temper like a kiln, but

Talk is cheap, a naira equivalent

- She is a Delilah! A half-empty

Mug shrouded in fine linen,

Threadbare yet unaware,

The splitting sight of Eve,

But for the towel wrapped

In rote to flower a man's

Man nature. Make no mistake,

It is noise after moans,

Malice after exhortation,

Then conciliation without

Necessity: an endless drudge.

So, brother open your eyes!

Tonney Ibe

THE BLACK BOULDER

Black are these echoes

Resonating

From the plagued trenches

-Pitch-black ;

The good and the bad,

Lost and losing the peace;

On bellicose fronts

- A campaign of untruths-

From the breaking black boulder.

We hear the faint crowing of the cocks,

Whose escape of murderous axes

Harangues on a liberal horizon,

At the trite entree of dawn.

Black is the jugular of the jejune jaguar,

Staring triumphantly at the spoils,

Black is the greed in antiquity.

Black is the light of truth

Long interred in sworn secrecy,

In a universe uninterested.

From an unintended peephole,

A thin ray of distant stars

Journeys in the hope of liberation;

Only one dark dot on the nether greens,

A trench flooded, a peopled gourd askew!

Dark-black madness of voices,

Relegated to self-made guillotines

- Ill at ease!

Black is the stagnation,

Flowing in a constant corruption

Against the deep; the eschatological;

The darker 'denges' posing in ignominy!

Black is the succinct sadness,

And the joy that could've been.

Black is the cause and effect

In this broken boulder!

MANTLE

I shall not be Okigbo,

I shall not be Marx,

I shall not be Luther,

I shall not be Guevara:

I shall be one in all.

Ut omnes unum sint

Is the mantle of the revolutionary.

LEVITATION

If I had wings,

I'd fly away in many ways

Not because I could, but

For the reinvention of my

Soul, the recreation of possibilities, and the release of

The human spirit in unison, as

I flip taking a leap out of this physical universe,

Into a superhuman multi-verse,

Where hunger, wanting, lack, plenty, pain and desire,

Vanish like rough edges on polished mahogany;

From there into the conurbation

Which exists fathoms beneath human essence.

If I had some wings,

I would soar not unlike a

Desert eagle, and perhaps tinker

With the idea, that freedom is

The root of bondage in which

Pursuit humanity is ever constricted.

But when I come to, from the wide

Stream of consciousness, I may yet

Realise that I, with mankind together,

Had titanium wings all along in the

Iron will inborn, innate yet inert.

If I knew I had wings,

I would spread the word throughout

The mystical ellipses of our Earth,

That all spirit eyes of spirit beings be

Open to the simple truth, that

The full gravity of this floating fleeting

World is subject to mind over matter.

Then I'd fly away to myself in search

Of nothing more but the tendering of my soul.

CATACOMBIAN

All paths lead underground, mankind walks on thin ice, so say the sticklers of the Word. From the advent of first weeping, the story begins.

Bound by ethereal forces, the lousy adventurer comes to notice the complexity of their plight: A long, or longer whisper to pledge the troth to chthonic and otherworldly gods. An indelible rut!

The curse is the rut of obeisance to the culture of a birth, and man a worshipper of the abstracts, plies a private trail in a private maze. It is a haunted carriage, prodded by ghostly voices reverberating within and without the lean length of feet, soul, and body.

The foreign god is local authority, omnipresent, the all-wise interlocutor. They are thunder, brimstone and the dove. Love ever inchoate is at war with The Love of The Voice, a locket and breaker of locks, the great Amistad from Bristol, to the proud wavelengths of uncharted isles.

Mankind must choose between darkness and Light, some prefer night to day, it comes down to choice. Ifa is the black creed, and the witch doctor is an ally not unlike Jesus who has come and died and risen and come again on the right hand of the right heart, somewhere on the aorta and ether of mortal consciousness, the histrionic blackmail endures.

Eight thousand feet high on a brown rock in Nepal a monk bereft of cheer looks to the east, an avuncular smile creasing his mug. A million head-bowing to the moon, or Ka'aba, could slightly avail his reservations.

It is set!: Mankind is the cursed blessing circumscribed to a catacombian voyage. Death, the passport, is the last port in the catacombs.

THE PLUNGE

Plunge me into temptation,

That I may mole my way

Through the labyrinths.

Sever all my fancy inhibitions,

The bloated clothing of skin

Overlaying a scalded soul,

So that I a mere mortal

Might be hanged by the mob.

Teach me to teach the joys of

Falsehoods over the red Sahel,

The forthright Babel of black,

Blue musings to the flawless.

Stay, sway, and slay the trumpeter

Who insists that purity is real.

My soul is a Sahara bedeviled

By ghosts and ghouls

From fifty-eight lifetimes.

It is hungry, thirsty, deeper

Than hell without a Sun;

Insanity a bouquet on the curb

Is but a victim of the continuum:

A mind of skulls skulking

To the infinite borders of history

-This tree of mystery within

The shallowness of perfection,

Must sooner catch on.

In the eye of the lighted wick,

The truths of tomorrow lie

Greater than all circumscription.

I am as you say,

Sinner and heathen beaten

On a beaten path a pact stricken,

With your higher senses

On this rollercoaster of mind.

You and they - we - see

That erring is a soulful airing.

HARBINGERIUS

Like a pen stricken of ink,

My tear-filled eyes no longer blink.

My heart is so heavy,

Buzzing as bees in a bevy.

Truth's, in fine, a harbinger of pain,

A grim release from the fruitless grain.

On and on, a soul must go,

Thro' and thro' the travails, and so

Consanguineous, Iscariot, or not,

Every life is a make-up of sorts.

The arrows puncture at my trust,

Perching upon these doubts that rust.

I shout aloud in silenced grief,

Into hollow abstraction - a sober relief;

Wary of a sibling's stabbing smile(s),

Vigilant as a groom on the aisle:

107

For blood seldom did, now it bends,

It's hard to tell who is a friend,

And if soothsayers serve a harsh dish,

Clarity reveals the darkest wish.

Brutus was a man - Caesar's undoing -

Harbingerius, a family fiend, subtly suing.

ADDICTION

Behind closed doors and shut slats,

A ghostly aura subdues sanity.

Images slide slowly on a wall's Private

Viewing of recorded sex scenes.

Between brief pauses of breath-catching,

Long hard hard-ons, absent contemplation,

And idle succumbing to the lower powers,

The soul loses touch with itself

Slipping into labyrinths of irremediable

Addiction to drugs on dial.

Beneath a blazing three-blade fan

Dancing to cool his rising temperature,

Sweats, lustily affirming a slavery

- A melon bulb of a head, heavy

As it's most likely to be.

Wading through the swamps, lost

Yet not wandering - in the room.

Even as bright LED lights bring

Forth full doses of advancements,

There is incomprehensible darkness

- The new Pandora's box by a click,

Unleashing upon the soul portable

Perdition, scary but never too swift:

Incomprehensible not irrepressible!

As the hands must leave the crotch,

There's proof that sighs were sighed

Between reality and virtual reality,

On the despoiled laps,

A semi liquid seminal sap,

Reduction, up for disposal.

On this path, the end is death!:

Some doors are entry-only,

Half-fulfilled in futile exits

Certainly drained of more

Than gratification could ever give.

In this doom of a tunnel.

Lust is sweet; sex sweeter,

Parallel to the grim reaper,

Pornography is the new addiction,

But In all addictions, there's hope.

HELL

From the four corners of the fire,

Accept this contrite offering,

This micro canto of purgation.

The Sweat's breaking the dust of earth,

Acknowledge it before the damnation.

Hell is this heaven for helots,

The Pseudo- cultural slaves

- Virile workers of the rural race.

Hell! Hell is the cost of our obsolescence;

The lunatic mosquito fattened in famine

Which feeds the millionth flame at moon time.

Incompetence is hell! This hell,

Though competent enough to give hell,

Is our incompetence.

You Wiseman with foolscap,

How long ago did we leave off,

112

Setting sails on a raft to the wilderness?

Such pride; such arrogance,

For the distant land long a coming - here!

This, here, is the hell talked about.

Hear! Listen to the inner voice,

Before all conscience is wooed by the furnace,

Turned to embers for the stockpile.

Hell is here, where we are!

Where ceiling fans collect dust

- Like bean collectors at a Mexican harvest -

Paralyzed from electric inactivity.

It is the currency of obsolescence,

Thighs ajar like the colossus

Beckoning upon first-class ills

In the third tier, last year; this year!

Hell is the death of progress,

Evidenced by the flying Agbadas

Of the peacocks,

Draping a hollow gaping emptiness.

Hell is you and I

Silenced and silent.

It's the pain you feel right now,

And the feeling unquantifiable.

Hell is awareness and unawareness!

We're in hell until we die.

CHIP OF ROCK

Earth is a sick pile,

The heart of man multiplied.

Love is the endangered species,

Peace by piece bound in stasis.

Behind the brilliant masque,

Smiles of deep magenta, is

The lone image of a weary soul.

Crucified by hugs and kisses,

And steamy passionate love-making,

The guise falls to centre, emboldened,

Lies thicker than ten Novembers,

Tears, regrets, the crackling embers,

This face, this severed soul is

Open to a dusty earth of tempests.

It is the earth, now and tomorrow,

Now, a chiseled chip of rock.

FELA

I love to choke,

Like Anikulapo,

To carry death in my pouch.

I know it sounds crazy,

But I can't help it;

I love crazy too.

While the world

Hopes to never die,

I long to remember my death:

Song of Bafouka ;

Song of revolution;

Song of the rebellion,

Slamming to the fear

Of irate camouflages:

The menace of thieves

Self-sufficient upon jazz

And Afrobeat, sultry sounds

Bang-bang-banging the

Naked gyrations of pain

In a million pidgin notes.

Fela is a dirge of history;

Ours stolen long ago.

MAMMON

Come now Mammon,

Bend the knee before scum.

Tonight is a festival of flavours!:

Three princesses and vodka,

Ham, honey, juice in jar;

Chat away a fresh apocalypse.

Tonight I claim your throne

And bash it to bits of bone;

I teach you politics,

Singing sorry songs of Amistad;

Tonight you are Abacha,

Moping and groping

On the king size mattress.

A slave, slippery as salmon,

Your destiny is my appetite

Steaming on the stove.

You are dinner forever,

And I a famished tyrant.

SURVIVOR

I hear church bells ringing

- In my head!

A muezzin's call at Maghreb,

Between the Baba casting Ifa:

 Cowry white and kernel black.

It is a war of the right-brain!

A survivor, I'm here, charged

With the weight of ciphers.

There are a ladder too many

To Supreme Intelligence:

A mortar of rungs,

A rigid footing of foots

Traversing the truly unknown.

All ayes are but near the half.

My head is a theatre,

And I, a survivor,

Observe and create.

ENIGMA

I know this:

I am an enigma

Mooning on the brim

Of lunacy, popping pills

Like pollen grains transfer

From anther to stigma by

The altruism of butterflies

Too hooked to acknowledge.

Whilst stigma steams between

Openings and closings of my

Shutters, I fill me up with

Colours of clouds full of rain

And pain. I am an artist,

Twenty-two seconds from implosion.

Shall I self-destruct, a casualty

Of the polity and her politics?

I am a passenger,

This much I know,

A private addict battling to break

The circle of generational grouse,

Envy, hate, fear, greed and avarice.

I render this confession on leaves,

Chafing on the sandy skulls of

Ancestors, sipping palm juice from

The wooden hollow of a Fiayenku

Calabash; but I am not proud,

Staring at the expanse of Olokun's

Massive ocean - all is numb in Walden.

I concede: I am one of the lost!

DISTORTED

Where's my handgun,

Let me put this one to sleep?

The smoker; the sinner;

The joker. the winner.

The air is foul,

Rank with the negatives,

The very point, untenable;

One less tragic hero then, who

Banters about other tragedies.

We are the world!

In this beautiful graveyard,

Rising high with high rises,

Birds will come home

As the crowd goes home:

Birds will come home

As the crowd goes home.

I want to go home!

THE WIND BLOWS

The wind blows

Bold and brave

Revealing the fowl's rump.

A flesh only flesh fresh,

To all things natural is

Guilty - guilty, filthy from

Ejection to expiration.

Upon the wind a slave's

Bound to please lest it tells

It to the world again and again.

This fowl, this man, shall someday

Master what it means to master

The wind - a sweep of spirits -

Coming from all corners,

Ruling the phantom self,

A chariot, a harlot, gusto

Stretching to the other side.

Immortality, a lifetime in

Immorality, is the only creed

Which led his rump to the tomb.

Alas an epitaph, tears, eulogies:

Blasphemies! By the swishing

Of a distant-traveled wind,

Life became as life intended:

Tears, the beginning;

Tears, the ending.

Tears within, without,

From eyes and rump.

The wind blows!

THE BARGE

Love came to her on a seaworthy barge,

The only stockpile, barrels overflowing;

A crake, a dove, the albatross.

She slew all but one.

In the knowledge of self, she won and lost.

Love then came to her,

Howling on elephant mountains

Like a wolf pack on a full moon

- She loathed the shrieking,

With hissing and sighs of irk.

She was the wolf, the barge, the albatross,

She was love running from itself.

Alone and in need of herself,

She's scampering on the greens

For a pound of the earthed treasury.

She is whatever you say she is.

WHERE I EXIST

There was light after a

Kiss from a queen of darkness,

One so bright it could've been

Channeled from the Sun. This

Light, nothing like the darkness

Often told in lore, a panoply

Of purity, pure madness, and

Sensuality; in one simple kiss

- To change a whole lifetime;

Then a tiny speck of gloom,

In the room in which from another

Room, vibrations of inspiration

Bounced off to less happy kisses.

If a kiss could gleam so much,

Why not joy thereafter, why not

Inspiration, and love in the light?

Light in darkness must run

Through the mill, wheeling out

127

Gardens of gardenias and roses.

So that the battles of doubt,

Under the light at the exit of tunnels;

One campaign after another staged

By a tiny speck on the tiny stage,

Were waged: raging raving hearts,

Spellbound in its vertigo.

Now this

Is

Where I exist!

Perhaps love from the kiss,

- On her dark lips -

Listless; doubtless, regardless,

Is a sought-after ravine

Gathered at a harvest of pillaged hearts.

Perhaps...the light,

Was (is) a cue to mark a point

Of entry, tearing through the fog where

Unpaired lovelies await the match.

Perhaps!...The kiss tranquilized and

Tranquilizes still all victim-souls.

Like quicksand, I sink slowly

Within, without, and beneath, putting

Paid to the succumbing fad.

Let there be light!

For now, this

Is

Where I exist:

In the kiss!

COURAGE

It takes balls to withstand

The horrors of the night,

Night of infinite lore lurking

As shadows of a powder keg,

Yearning for fire elemental

In the great storytelling;

Fractured tall tales spoken,

A toast to perfection:

Olympus,

Forever unattainable!

There's little luck for man,

Man the puppet-pawn

Captured by the illusions

And delusions of a grand plan.

The human soul is a vacuum,

Nature all its own,

An earth in motion spun

To melodies with maladies:

Life a big fat cake for

Ten decades of sleepwalking,

The knife to swipe to bits

Every splinter till the last.

Such is the sibilation

Within the psyhcal plexus

Floating between inner space:

A milky way of stars

Turning to the knowledge,

To the truth of true man

So given to platitudes

- Sermons on the harp

Of ears; of flesh and skin.

The horrors of the night

Lay low like cavemen

Camped in a five star suite,

Every day in the glitter, a

Sacrificial lamb to polish.

Unabashed hypocrisy is rife

Playacting from gutter to lips ,

The sacred base downplayed;

Gracious gifts of imperfection

Languishing on the gallows,

Spitting at world wisdoms!

The wisdom of reflections

Is sterile to possibilities of

Warped refractions of light.

Blind to angelic dusts

In the fully blown demon.

What nature to embrace,

Horrors of the night!

YOU

Your talent is gasoline,

But you are the spark.

Set the world afire,

The constructive destruction

Is a return to Eden:

Eden lost in the painting,

Warped by ideologies,

Born anew in you.

Singe this waste

Of Oceans and deserts,

To preserve the mangroves;

To tame man the animal;

To reassure the animal kingdom.

There's dirt in the hearth

Piling to the hilt.

You were born to destroy!

A POET'S PLIGHT

It is a blessing to preside

Upon the assemblage of words

Straight from the ether: to see disorder

Coming into its own; as they

Sojourn through the half-mad mind

Which is unfortunate to pick the frequency.

The sum of mental rumblings register

From the mentalities of man-beasts to the

Eccentricities of ordinary souls indulging

In extraordinariness; in the mind of the

Bard, who bears the cross without grudge

To some place of skulls in his assaulted

Personage, never to find the old self again.

But it is hard to be a poet when worms

Whine within the depth of oneself,

Striking monotonous chords in hunger.

It is a drudge to think of

Words and daily bread, for muses gift

Truths, not fruits. With some hope-filled

Promise, they tell of a rich cornucopia

At the end of the tunnel of tribulations:

The poet knows better!

What manner of words whoosh out

Of a positive heart fraught with sterile

Dreams - unsatisfied - incapable of

Advancing a valid check in the

Physical world of capitalism, far away

From the literary box of trances?

When his pot is clogged with cobwebs

- A canvas of communism - is it worthy

Of a song? Who takes care of inspiration

Personified? Some pray to see another day,

To wallow in hedonism again, but

If tomorrow never comes it would be

Fine, except for tomorrow where the poet

Exists as lord of the manor's stretch:

A burgeoning republic of sorts where

His dreams sit stolidly on solid ground.

He favours the best fasts - fasts of

Rediscovery - dipping the mind-pen deep

Into a metaphysical poultice of metaphors,

Madness, and socio-personal rebirth;

His self becoming a prisoner of his art. Yet,

In between the lengthy masses of his travails,

His wellbeing dictates the wellness of his craft.

The poet needs love!

TRUTH AND THE NOOSE

Like a wingless Phoenix,

She arises and flies

From the parchment of all things.

She, a ladybird,

Averse to aimless chirping,

Sings against the reins:

The noose and the soul,

In incoherent accord,

Exchange a thousand gazes

Before the brief marriage.

She soars undaunted still,

Unfazed by the sentences

Nor the sententious judge;

Spits at the blind rope

Deafened by noise of its stringing,

Choking on itself.

She curries in the sun,

Light as a fig brush,

137

Lightly; sharply,

Into the doom of what is,

In constant conflict

With what ought to be.

She may be both!

A fire to a noose,

But a noose in herself.

She wearies the hunter,

Little knowing

She never left his side.

She is...,

Spark for a cigar;

Nourishment for a soul;

Eyes for a body;

Fact for a fiction:

The fiction of a soul,

A body and a cigar,

Like ink to a pen,

The pen which writes

A litany of laws,

Buttonholing

An unsuspecting wanderer;

Spears at his urges,

And desires and bents.

She's a painful comfort,

For the fortunate eccentric.

She says:

"You're an ocean of imperfections;

Wisdom and folly,

The benthos of your being."

Unstoppably she stares,

At the noose and the noosing.

Undeniably, she endures.

WOMAN

A woman is like a cloud,

A body of water,

Moving in flotation.

Her eyes are deep yet shallow,

Not unlike fire, they burn

Into the soul of the attracted.

Vain by nature,

She's troubled by her looks,

Lending ear to the fancy talker:

If he sings the songs she likes,

He may fall into her favour; but

The favoured are few and far between

- She is both!

She is Earth!

She rotates on her axis

With a unique girth.

In payn and joy

She rolls along:

The perfect boy!

A woman is beauty,

Purity and truth:

The spoor of cherubs on tour.

Her passion cannot be slaked,

Yet the gallant must try!

Her heart's a sleeping dragon:

Tamed by love,

Its every breath's a pleasant haze.

Taunted by betrayal,

Her fires eagle at the tormentor

In a dirty vengeance.

She's the poster image of the world

(The world as it's known),

Though that which was before

Is yet still here as beauty.

She's that world internalized,

Coded by the godhead(s)

141

- Never to be fully understood.

A woman is imperfection,

And imperfection is life!

Her stomach's an anachronism,

Relevant, Significantly spiritual.

It sheaves out

Constructors and destructors:

It's the nadir of tomorrow!

With a tongue marinated in honey,

And spices from the ethereal Orient;

She carries power in her purse,

Ever reminded, as she applies makeup,

Of what dynasty she belongs.

She is a blessing

Awaiting its target.

One day at a time,

The blessed ones confess.

She's an ocean of oceans,

An onion sea of depths.

She loves to be pampered with words,

Peppered with tenderness;

Driven to the highest mountains.

A bridge of love and beauty,

She's both!

A maze of sorts,

Yet she cries sometimes,

Tears not of vacant sorrow!

 So she smiles in payn,

Grinning in the traps of joy.

If all women are loved unconditionally,

Earth shall rediscover love anew;

Its force may parry all misnomers.

For in her wrath evil is beautiful,

And beauty becomes evil.

It rises like a king Cobra,

Many times before the final strike;

Rehearsing its contentions

In a session of doom.

143

(She's) an enigma,

Therefore the world might be so.

We are who she appears to be:

To be a woman is to be much!

DESTRUCTOR

Give me Eve

And a pleasant garden,

I will write a Utopia;

I will tame the serpent;

I will study the tree,

And make more gardens.

Paradise begins

In my lemongrass backyard,

Where Eve walks naked,

Palms bearing orange juice

For better possibilities

Like Abel without Cain

Amongst Abels and Cains.

I am Adam

The Weaver unaware

That his destiny is destruction.

LIFE

The cradle

Is

But

A distant memory.

In the mirror

A grave,

A box;

A promise of eternity.

Innocence

Is

A miscarriage:

The spattered

Blood of purity

- Stillborn.

The end a beginning,

Six-feet

For the guilty.

A memory: a memory!

A MAN LIKE JOB

You advance the trails of Melchizedek,

Mantellettas adorning your mahogany closet;

In the light and lightning of uncommon truth,

But are you a man like Job?

With suavity beyond compare,

Persuasive psychology and seductive Latin,

The columns of Jericho jingle to your echoes,

But ask yourself, are you a man like Job?

It's ominous your future is bright,

For the sun swaggers in the monarchy of faith,

And you an exorcist, a scrupulous cleric,

Are bound to bask in celestiality.

So when personal pestilence strikes,

Deserted and derided by foe and friend,

Lucifer with divine Carte Blanche,

Can you be a man like Job?

ARE WE ALL ACTORS!

Although I write, I'm no writer,

Although I sing, I'm no singer,

And oh! I lead but I'm no leader,

Yet I try to be these things.

In a lifelong rainbow of make-belief,

I and others very much like me,

Rehearse our inimitable character,

Disillusioned by the idea of perfection:

Sometimes a tragedy, other times not,

As we try to understand that

Neither tragedy nor comedy lasts forever.

The dramaturge drafts,

Change becomes the dramatis personae!

I know now that I'm no writer,

Singing while I lead, I am neither,

For how could I be these things,

When they task against my volition?

I wonder:

Do we all want to be actors?

PSYCHAL WATERLOO

An aching voice thunders, 'get up!',

Like the Oriental Magi, I follow

Into the glee and gloom of my own.

A blind soul, a mind bemoaned, a belabored body!

Stuck in a prison of no trivial temptation,

I lord over my basest limitation(s).

A nightmarish night, starless skies, mute screams!

The revelations impress upon me:

How is it I preside a priori upon

My cluelessness and utter oblivion?

When my guardian angels flee,

My soul quavers, I'm unlike me;

Hope seems an unavailing liability.

A flesh defiled, destiny deserted, a soul in ferment!

My spirit discords in every profanation.

Vanity victories over mortal intelligence,

149

Before a parallel of spirituality;

And the proud distraction of belief,

Makes it a fad ever so believable.

While we quest for the flaming light,

We forget that we keep it out of sight.

All men are born vain but unaware!

TO THE ASHES

Here lies a weary soul,

Numb and dumb

The breathless body,

Ripe for hell again - or bliss.

At last, peace is come!

By no pricking of the sword;

No poking of the heated colt,

The journey of spice

Has whistled the final denouement.

No more panting;

No more chanting;

No more soft touches,

No more fears nor cares

- No more!

The cross is circled

On an ebbing of the tide.

From dust to life,

The drudge of strife,

To the kumbayya of maggots,

The proud man who laughed

Twelve dozen times

Lies motionless, a faint eclipse of

Earthly accomplishments on the weeping

In heavy hearts and telling eyes.

In the music of the moment,

A million muses make merry

To the apotheosis,

This dearly departed, several seasons

A message imparted in the marketplace

Of sighs and grins of highs and lows.

Here lies the most profound fool,

Whose private life was Pandora's Box.

The still and uneasy man,

A thousand souls - legion -

Demons whose fisticuffs

Met the final round.

His mind, a cave uncharted,

In life and life-after, soars

Beyond the vase,

Beyond the urn,

Beyond the chest-like cage

Where all free spirits

Find their chains unchallenged.

Here lies the perfect module

Of imperfection, singing

In a lighter dimension

The same songs of his youth:

The sum of his span!;

The charlatan who wrote.

The words like wings

Flapped and flung into the distance,

To freedom and intermittent relief,

Have brought him here

- The vacuum of entities -

Here the pot of ashes:

The climax and anti-climax!

In the surfeit of flowers

For the conviction on a fated passing,

Cheers to the ashes

That was the enigma

EKO: WAR CAMP

Battles for self-preservation are

Fought, in silent detonation

Of explosives as passers by

Stride - high hopes hanging -

On a tainted thread dragging

Blurry memories in the making,

Made to suit the setting.

There are no tents here, only

Tarpaulins for the nonce:

Soft spots 'ere beers blow,

Splashing to pacify all restive

Souls who may slug the ale

- Travelling to a distant revelation.

What a somber victory it must

Be, to own a fount in famine!

An unearned relief to hound;

But Justice is forever yawning!

Pride is the vanity of a fool,

Eko is her ancient archer:

A war camp of the Bini,

Of axes, jujus, and machetes;

Where Osun are still in birth;

The coastal quarters of nascent

Prospects, immorality, and

Starved wishes. Eko...indeed!

The focus is the raging war, not

The carcasses of several sacked

Dreams, whose ashes as before

Soar on the stomach of sad black

Rivers beneath beautyful bridges,

Housing a horde of hoodlums.

Sadly...sadly...sadly!

The overground is an underground

Of dust and depression; fumes

And frustration, and inspiration.

She's a concrete cemetery, for

Which the holy and quasi-holy

Compete, to the unbiased umpire.

Her culture endures invasion, yet

Centuries after the occupation,

Her back's become flooded

With a colony of complexions,

And the sounds of selfish sirens

Beaming, booming, and bustling.

A promiscuous mother in her prime,

Her milk's ever in short supply,

With breasts understaffed for

The plenitude of drooling mouths;

But true to circumstances,

She welcomes pained labour

Unloaded at motor parks,

Factories and market piers.

Therefore despite herself, she

Yearly intercedes to Olokun for

Salt, fish, sand, and commerce;

Celebrating the Eyo'o in white,

Masked in silk and top hat,

Resonating antithetic flashes of

The shrieking Egungun.

'Tis the same war camp, but an

Altogether different battlefield

- Of transient white flags!

In those gay-laden windows,

Amnesia's earned in laughter,

After wine and skilled preachers

- Leaders of the militias -

Word all of the pain away,

Like a vicious capitalist,

Pushing the will of conquest.

So from swamp dwellings, to

Banana Island mansions, froth

And posturing are gradated.

But all the same, she

Tells some telling truths:

Poverty is an incomplete burden,

Wealth a constant escape;

Envy is a perennial seed,

Watered by itself it seems,

Inviolate when it's fruited,

Roots spread sturdily below;

Violence is a fact of life

- Her life, legal or illegal!

The most insolent soul's an

Alpha sampling the choicest

Largesse, criminality of the

Commonality as commonplace as

The Oligarchs', Eko's a wounded

Heaven- a hemophiliac bliss,

Pricked by floral daggers of her

Own majestic beauty in bondage.

All those who walk upon the

Stagnant mother at night, are

Stagnated themselves in full

Light. They are unafraid

Because they've much to fear.

In Eko, Justice is a blind

Drunk, who in infrequent

Sobriety, might be just though

Bad wine is a good liar!

There's a church beside a

Mosque beside a shrine

- Business is in the bloom;

She, a fine disease of home!

Cultural curfews seize star

Times, sweepin' thro' serpent

lines, as a reminder to

The downtrodden that

Everyone is a suspect;

Yet under the flame of

Taboos, half-nude nymphs

Validate red disco lights,

Wiggling Mama's gifts to

The most proper pocket.

From all walks of life, the

Clientele troops in and out,

And back again on Eko's

Back - on the war

Path - home.

There are no pillories for

Thieves, save an errand

To the netherworlds, by

Bastinadoes of the mob, as

So many saw not a

New day in heeding

The Stomach Anthem,

To the daft wrath

Of a few foolish men.

It is in many a sense,

Becoming clear as blue

That the pen is a

Great greedy thief;

And fast fingers on

Laptop keys, the sum

Of a hundred Machiavells

- She inspires inspiration!

If there's a ghetto, then

There are no uptowns;

Only rich and poor slums

- And there are ghettos!

Eko's some excellence,

In the jaws of perdition

- A dashing disaster, where

No one is not a victim!

She is still and always

Will be a war camp.

BIZARRE CANTILLATIONS

Chapped lips, tart mind,

On the edge

Of the brink;

On the sink

For the dredge,

puffing, praying, pouting;

Sipping, shirking, slipping!

Though-out trees stretching,

Posterity for the nesting;

Avernus-bound savouring

Counter-Nirvana:

Pumped-up castles in the air

Descending!

Pray you, this heart,

Into the light;

Pray you, this soul,

Assent to levitation;

This sinister slice as one,

Into stiff-ear latency;

The world in witness

To the Primordial Painting.

Oh the humming!

The Sopranos drumming;

Broken mirrors - testamental!

Bizarre cantillations chanting,

Like pseudo-Lucifer psalms,

Conceding, they accede

To needless exorcism.

Chapped lips -serpentine;

Tart mind -foolhardy;

Restless soul uncomfortable!

Two eyes star-gazing

Through sunup staring,

A body nowhere out here.

Bizarre Cantillations,

Into the light come,

On History's breasts,

Fragments

Of a visitor's reflections.

II

CONFESSIONS

CROSSROADS

We are at a crossroads, you and me,

At the center of joy and jaded pain;

Eye-crossed, heart-locked, palm-in-palm

From an unsure distance.

In my dreams I kissed you

A million times - lips entangled, untangled,

Entangled again. I need you,

I need a miracle, a timely watershed;

I need heaven on this crossroads.

In an alley left of forever,

I see you, purity,

Chastity; the colour of the rain,

You are my rainbow of passion.

We are at a crossroads,

On our way to decision,

I hold your hands like a tame wildebeest,

You follow, you follow and follow.

165

I love to think I love you,

To kiss the thought of your thoughts.

You give me fever, I want it; I want you.

From this crossroads we shall evolve,

You and I, my love!

I

This room is a pungent vacuum,

No more the smell of paradise,

No more, no more,

Now that you are away.

Goodness! I'm a stickler for touch,

If, only if, touch means your soul

Touching mine, slowly,

All over my centerpieces,

Slowly, just like that, the last time,

Pleasure was the sum of it all.

When are you coming home,

Right here where the heart beats?

When shall we fly again,

Across the shores of Lagos

Hands adjoined in the air?

Come, fill this room once more

With laughter, madness, and craving.

Come, just come,

With that fragrance of life,

Save me from the drought.

Till then, these walls

Are only blocks of lime.

Till then, these walls

Mess with the mind.

I miss you.

II

Your skin is falsetto,

The tempo

Of ultraviolet rays;

It is magnetic:

Drawing me in,

A blunt shear,

I scrape slowly,

Sweetly, helplessly.

Take me apart

Or put me to task,

In your field of allure

I roost and reel,

A troubled prisoner.

III

I may never find love,

But I can look into your eyes,

I can caress your hair:

Every soft strand

In every finger of my hand.

I could kiss your forehead,

Your neck, both your ears,

And watch you fall asleep

Wherever you wish on me.

My heart's been whispering,

Ministering to you, goddess;

It sings, it sings, it clings

To the scent of freedom,

And the promise of pain.

It must be love,

But who has found it?!

Beauty is least of the props,

The perfect waistline,

Nor thighs of Ghanaian gold

All fall short of the flight

To abstraction, in and out

Of two souls hungry for salt.

Your breath is death,

Pure and simple, and

I walk on the pike

Set for destruction:

I may not find love!

IV

I live for candlelight moments

Under the stars,

The music of peace on repeat.

I long for love,

For life,

For pink butterflies

Fluttering in the movements

In the moments,

Up and down my soul.

Who is a soul mate,

A better half,

A capsule of love,

A life partner?

Love is the green porch

In the night,

A picnic for two,

The melody of a being.

I long to go deep,

To feel alive,

To come alive,

And dance the dance of life

Without drama

V

She shines,

From head to toe

A rhyme.

Lips of Pandora;

Ice-cold,

Peppery soul.

She is a thorn,

A hot bomb

Moments away from reality.

She is a fiend,

Delilah, Jezebel,

A dull-edged Cleopatra.

Her world is beauty,

And beauty is not enough.

AMOR

Love is a soul dreaming

Or a heart screaming.

It almost came

Till it came to.

The heart knows!

Every rejection is acceptance,

Every frown full of hope.

A smile I smiled,

A laugh I laughed,

I hopped and bumped and jumped

When it was young and stupid.

Then a weak teardrop,

Betrayal,

Forgiveness,

The bearing of witness.

Insight is inside

The weight of knowledge,

In pain overflowing.

The mire called desire,

A taste of quagmire.

Love is levitation

Straight into the sky,

The best high.

A hug I hugged,

The cause I bought,

My God!

Truths were little lies.

Love without vision

Is a fickle admission.

Love is blind, and

Blue behind the blinds.

I crouched, I crawled,

And leapt no more

Than a toad in labour.

How swiftly change comes

Sweeping through

Angels and demons:

Each becoming the other!

Love is compatibility,

Rejection biding the time.

It is a fated break

For a lesson.

It is a taming till the fading,

Emptiness,

Infinite black nectar;

A beast unleashed

Havoc unhanded,

Rebranded:

The bees disbanded!

It is a dream.

VI

The first time I saw you

My soul couldn't stop

To pee. I was wet,

All the way to my mind.

You were the bulb

Shining so brightly in

My dreams and nightmares.

Ten years in one minute,

I could see the prophecy.

You, a splash of mother,

Grandmother, grand mistress,

I was born to meet

- On that unpleasant day -

And believe in Paradise.

One look, one connection,

A touch, a torch further in;

I imagine dancing with you

In a maze of flowers and

Death is all I wish.

If life could be this perfect,

Life after must be perfection.

You've always dwelled

In my soul, a splice of me,

The whole of you;

Your gutters,

Your marketplaces,

Your dirty and clean,

church and shrine.

Every kiss is worship,

Every touch a praise,

Your knees, the keys

To a stream in perdition.

You approve, and I swim,

Natural, naturally

To your heart.

Because of you I love hell,

Pain, betrayal, and more.

I am a helpless snail

Under your spell,

I can tell.

VII

Right now all I can think about

Is the world beyond your lips.

Atlantis:

I would be lost,

A Mayan without arms.

But you are you,

Thunder and brimstone

Clapping rare gemstones

On your lap of sap.

By sleight of hand ,

I fear what I'm fated to be:

Jack Sparrow,

Pirate of your seas;

Rugged interloper

Walking on White sharks,

 Into the darkest deeps

Where Hades is a wave

To redemption.

It is only your lips,

Pink and soft like mink.

In my heart I built you

A modest parsonage,

The keys your kisses

I have failed to find.

Life may yet be a dream,

A long scene

Of laughter and screams.

I know for I have dreamed,

It began with your lips.

A PENNY FOR YOUR LOVE

A penny for your love,

My dear,

For a time with you;

Take this penny: me,

Upon your favourite hill.

A penny for you!

For the pleasure of your company;

A penny for your love:

That pure lava straight from God;

To burn away my soul's darkness.

You showed me to my wings,

Behind that black Bohemian door,

Where they weaved with gossamer.

A penny and a kiss for you,

For you gave me your wings as well.

My soul says you are the one,

Created specially for me alone.

You've walked with me sweet thing,

In life, and death, and life again.

A penny for your penny, love,

My two pennies are all yours!

My light and my darkness,

My scarce and my plenty;

You share with me unconditionally.

You are my art! You see

How easily you become my life?

We make magic as we make love,

A thing of legend and folktale!

A penny for all of you,

To claim your kingdom in my heart;

A penny for your thoughts love:

Those high rise treasures of your mind!

A penny, a pound, a goldbrick,

You are, priceless as the sibilation

Of a Martian ocean.

You are my penny!

Countess! Duchess! Majesty!

You set me free!

A penny for your love,

My love!

VIII

In your facial frame,

Da Vinci is born again

The hand of God at work.

Attractive fires like

A lakeside bonfire splash

With sincere songs

From each bearing heart.

I confess that your smile

Is a potent world war

No Helen of Troy measuring;

A grin of cold ginger ale,

Teeth ushering in the Sun.

Oh dear, smile no more,

For my world's at risk:

A focused gaze as I

Graze on the cliff

To a gracious riff.

Smiling all the way

- I long to fall

In you!

MY LEAVE, I TAKE

In the sandstorm,

You came,

A fated whirl of wind,

And swept me off my feet.

The storm, over now,

Is a wave of hailstones

Below the deck of hearts

Where my soul salvation

Kissed: You're the storm!

Between brief happy bites,

The fights for nothing but

Lies and deceit, eat up an

Erstwhile healthy meal

That was us -you and I.

Shivering in this hurricane,

Drenched and condensed,

I wave the white banner

Fleeing like Lot from the

Twin cities in the eye

Of dystopia. I shall not

Be a chip of salt, nor

Matter for the cyclones.

I must walk an athlete,

A baton of white

For the joyful exchange

Which tomorrow promises.

I take my leave of you.

GARDENER

Curse my eyes,

For drawing from your beauty

The appreciation of art.

Your gait is a threat

To abstinence,

So I abstain -not!

Such is the entrance

To happy incontinence.

On your altar,

I confess, I confess!

Lust ensured the loss,

But I was lost

From the very beginning;

Your epic ellipses

Dug deep into...,

Top to bottom,

Back to rear,

Healing a blind man:

A million blessings!

I can see!

I see:

Two moons on an Iroko;

Two grand gourds by God,

A miracle outstretched

From seventh heaven,

Ending the droughts;

A desired fatwa,

Thus the dog-man leaps

At the golden bone!

One hymen, one accord:

One spiritual contract.

The trapdoor is trampled,

Paradise on the flip side.

So curse my eyes

- The blessed curse;

You are a rose garden,

The pride of mermaids.

For you, I have

Become a gardener.

191

IX

Kiss me but betray me first,

Betray away before trust,

Trust me enough to unveil

The Hera in your soul.

I am a mirage of perfection

A lot like you!

Love me inexpressibly,

In thrift, tears, and taboo.

I am yours to wrap ;

To smoke, to inhale and exhale:

Ashes fated as your weeping!

Beat me but stay,

Open fire - fire at will!

I, the bent papaya, love you.

You're a tunnel route

To paradise, and I

Became, to hurt and love you.

X

Beautiful love! If only you

Knew how much I love you,

Your eyes would breed an

Immoral offspring of Night

And Day.

Fine like an obscure Cinderella,

You tread the bestial path within,

Strolling aimlessly upon the Great

Wall erected by age-long familial

Feuds, spite, bad blood, and

Wide-eyed obsession for romantic

Security. I love you as heaven

Is my witness, but the weakness is

The shrew in your perfect soul.

Let the past be indicted for your flaws,

Let the moment give in as you concede,

Let the silent thunders rumble

And mark thusly this two-year

Passion, which became the object of

Mixed envy and half-professed

Admiration; let your heart key into

Mine, knowing fully well that truths

Were told spoken in the astral lingo.

No matter, in your deepest recesses

Understand, that I stand by you

Like Job awaiting a turn of the tide.

You'd tan the dark spots,

If you knew how much I love you.

XI

I see the webs,

Everywhere about,

Spiritual-, mental-,

Emotional-gossamers,

And walk head-on.

Your touch was the dream,

A haunting awakening

I see...You everywhere!

Like all rivers,

I know not where it leads;

Love, a river, is overwhelming!

But I dare to risk,

A life of swimming,

Swimming on the tides,

To you; in you; for you.

I am

A fool - your fool!

Now I see,

I came, a pitcher

In your web,

In danger and comfort

By fireside in the freezing.

Your voice has

Prised open

The world I seek;

Into the bargain

Reflections - sustained!

On the crest

Of this avalanche

You have stirred,

I realize,

It is you I love.

FIRST THINGS

Love was two innocent kids

Enamored of each other,

You and I, uneasy.

It was the forbidden!

I kissed you from afar,

Without the faintest clue

Of the meaning of a kiss;

Your lips a honeycomb

- I licked and licked and licked!

We stumped and stumped

On the old stomping grounds

Of innocence, you and I;

Two ordinary souls unfolding;

I, drunk on you,

You, a chimney of me;

We transcended ourselves!

Though the years prevail,

I sport memories of you,

A furtive revelation of God's

Gift to a dejected stone

Like me.

With joy in my soul,

I water a garden in my heart

For you.

Since the first things,

A gentle hello,

A smile, a hug,

A kiss: release!;

I became a prophet.

XII

A gaze like a maze,

She sets my soul aflutter.

Her eyes, two worlds rotating,

Hold me spellbound as the

First time I beheld the sea.

Woman of the veil!

I am the prisoner who knows

There is a God.

XIII

Oh woman!

How delicate is your tenderness!

The literature of your love is

So scholarly, you merit a Nobel.

Eighth world wonder,

I can only wonder who tailored

Such a magnificent design.

Bewitching as a crescent moon,

I am trapped, a werewolf

Forever human in your spell.

A new breed of seductive apples,

Must be the twin layers of your lips:

Kill me with your skills!

RASHIDAT

Love is God, from nothing came,

Spreading hope, lighting the flame

Of life in life till death's beyond,

And pleasured pain in bold neon.

A joy so pure; so fair, and tender,

From belly butterflies in slow surrender;

Trust, a careless arrow, blind; brown,

A slave and archer of bow and frown.

She was love's very constitution,

A splash of succour - a horror collision :

Angel and demon; snake and saint,

Caged in concert to never relent.

For to capture an image of her smile(s)

Of mischief, melody, and truthful guile,

The halved fraction of a moment

Is sweeter than justice to hellish torments.

201

Her hair - health in every strand,

No aphrodisiac outdoes the brand -

Mannered and tousled basking in wind,

Concocts tricks to marvel the mind.

Nubile Osun of the red Midwest,

Discarding hijabis to reveal the rest;

Struck by nature's electric shock,

Healed his heart of lifeless luck.

Belief was the Red Sea 'rever split,

Starving desire of the sumptuous meat.

She's married now for duty sake,

Both hearts condemned to never break.

XIV

When I look upon you,

I remember that

The sun rises in the east.

You heal me with a simple smile,

Lighting and piercing an impure

Porous soul. It is settled:

I am lost and found between

Your absence and presence.

I look to the east to espy the bloom,

I look to the west to see you rest.

Boy am I blessed to kiss, hold and hug

The sun in the flesh.

Beauty Is a rung of love,

And Love is all we need.

You're all that I require!

XV

A castaway, I sought solace

In your arms; your scent; your eyes.

Heaven was the kiss,

Hell the memory,

Sweet pain to kiss and remember,

A heart to enter;

The center to master!

I, the fugitive, run from commitment;

I, the renegade, the runaway;

I, the ingrate, the hunter, the gardener,

Am at a crossroads: to love, or

Love enough! O the humanity!

Loving you was easy,

But life is hard,

Harder to hold on...to

All, or nothing, of you.

I see the thunderbolts splaying,

A storm brewing beyond the blues.

I see me loving you

No further than a memory;

No further than this!

CLARIONICLE

I craved love but met obsession;

Meant companionship, got followership;

A gentle smile, a clownish laugh.

So now I dare not wish solitude,

Nor a heaven at least

Where my name is unknown,

Nor a life easy, simple and sublime.

It is all a waterfall!

Heaven seize this life of mine,

That satisfies a dream of surfeit;

Of wishes wired by wide clamours

Into a vacuum veiled unlike

Here - here, where I know.

A carnal fraud, a divine truth,

An exemplar of imperfections,

An African!: an African,

Mind, soul, spirit, flesh,

Contemned to chart in futility.

I long to be alone,

I sing a song all alone;

I would never be alone,

I see the cheering crowd.

The toil, the powdery satisfaction,

The transience, the fiction,

The tears and mounting fears.

Without a care in the nonce

For the many cares,

Without joy or joy alone,

Weary for wishes,

A human being emerges.

XVI

Looking at the candlelight

Lit in your netherworld,

I can't deny that I'm famished for

Deep laughter, sure sadness, true

Love and a full heart to share.

Save me, saving me a space

To breathe in the Summer breeze,

Kissing you endlessly, tenderly

On your soul - soul to soul -

A goal to score, in win or loss;

By the spiritual hearth ever burning.

You - are - my muse, look

The way of this hourglass:

My shattered soul - trickling

Ounce by ounce, lonesome for you.

I've saved all my love for you!

XVII

You deserve an Oscar

For the way you love me.

I know!

You really act it out,

professionally, naturally

The divine script as intended,

From the sweetest depths of you,

I know!

This thing called love's shining

All about your gestures.

Your smile is a dagger,

It cuts; it cuts clearly, cleanly,

Close to my soul, a spitting

Image of an enamored heart

Too far gone!

A beautiful dream, such is love,

A dream, only beautiful.

Sweet love, I'm still learning what love is.

XVIII

Take a kiss down the alley

Where love is a cactus garden,

Impress upon your insecure heart

Its watershed inscriptions. I tell

You, from my lips to your soul,

A kiss can change your life,

A kiss can mend your wounds,

A kiss can flower your porch.

Don't be shy or hard-hearted,

Love again, again, and again.

XIX

Let the winds blow about your ears and sing that I have tried.

Let my eyes beg like they were at the golden gate,

A flawed soul, I am trying, reeling to adapt.

Take me as I am, a profound novice,

A student, learning how love

Pries open goodly vistas.

XX

My drunk of a soul

Staggers in a psychal stupor

Listlessly over, and again,

In the lions' den. When, I

Wonder, shall the wandering end?

Love is in need of you and I:

I, a stickler for pain,

You, a distant hope by now,

Dancing with death

In the orchard of the beast.

Your love was the candlelight

That illumined my labyrinth-life.

Your love was the dark cloud

Which hung above my chains.

If wine must become patience,

Grapes must meet the harvest.

213

A thudding heart calling out

To you, I shall wait forever

Till then, or never,

When you see me by your side.

XXI

Today I love you,

No more than I always have,

Deeply we connect,

Deeper than the arrow's plunge.

"I love you! I love you! I love you!",

Lovers mime upon the peaks,

Washing it into a cliché;

But I love you

Truly, silently and spiritually,

In an abstract way

That words cannot express.

Because of you,

I know who I am.

And because of this,

I know who I could become:

A better person everyday!

You are my forbidden fruit!

For when I tasted you,

I kissed the scales goodbye.

I love you today,

Even more than yesterday,

Though no occasion ever

- Marriage, Valentine nor whatever -

Could valuate or validate my emotions.

Like mists upon the Kilimanjaro,

Your essence is cloaked in mystery;

Yet every step I take

- Against the white clouds -

Holds some promise of Canaan.

So I take these steps,

Fully aware that I might fall,

Into your imperfect story;

Because I know in the end,

That all my troubles bend

When I look into your eyes.

Today I love you as always,

But I celebrate you as well,

For I found you

Then I found myself;

And so if ever

I'm asked what heaven is,

I would lean on you,

And answer "like this!"

We're all like rainbow hues,

But some cannot see past the flesh,

Your every palette is a blessing.

It's one of many reasons why

I love you, babe.

Only time may tell,

How you truly make me feel.

I love you - for real.

XXII

Like some *Mene-mene* on your

Philistine wall-face, I bear testimony

As I hear you say you love me.

Neither prophet nor guru,

I know that I love you, and

Know Love which adults know:

It's trust, and trust, surrender;

It's power like the higher force,

Dangling within tempting height,

To adore, desire, taste and consume so

That another soul's subdued in rescue.

Yes! I know that I love you!

I hear the blues from your lips,

So reassuring, so soft, so Bob Marley!

And my doubts almost peter out,

Until your actions inspire more.

You are

Delilah in an angel,

Yet I,

Neither prophet nor guru,

Know hook, line and sinker:

I love you so.

CPSIA information can be obtained
at www.ICGtesting.com
Printed in the USA
FSHW021249300419
57715FS